SOUL SONGS

An Anthology

R.A. FALCONER

Words to Uplift, Restore & Inspire

Text copyright © 2018 Rachel Alana (R.A. Falconer).
First published in print and ebook 2025. All rights reserved.
The moral right of the author for copyright has been asserted.

Without limiting the rights under copyright reserved above, no portion of this book may be reproduced, stored in or introduced into a retrieval system, or transmitted in any form or by any other means, (electronic, mechanical, photocopying, recording or otherwise,) without prior written permission of the author and copyright owner, except as permitted by Australian copyright law.

Jacket and interior book design created by R.A. Falconer.
Background front cover base art: Nasiyat Akmatova, Canva full subscription license.
Editor B.C. Ballestrin.

Print ISBN 979-8-2843450-8-5 (Paperback. Amazon Ed).
Print ISBN 979-8-2854865-4-1 (Hardcover. Amazon Ed).
Print ISBN 978-1-7638544-1-3 (Hardcover. Ingram Spark Ed).
Print ISBN: 978-1-7638544-0-6 (Paperback. Ingram Spark Ed).

https://www.facebook.com/midwivesofthesoul/
https://www.instagram.com/midwivesofthesoul/

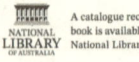

I wish to acknowledge the Kaurna Meyunna, the traditional stewards of the land on which this book was written. I wish to acknowledge the Elders, past and present, and the bridge both Aboriginal and Torres Strait Islanders uphold between this country's soul, wisdom, and spiritual history and the current, emerging culture. I pay respect to them, and all they have gone through.

They are this land's first storytellers.

SOUL
SONGS

*"An old alchemist gave the following consolation to
one of his disciples: 'No matter how isolated you are and how lonely
you feel, if you do your work conscientiously, unknown friends will
come and seek you.'"*

~ Carl Jung

This book belongs to those incredible souls who 'found' me when I was certain all seemed lost. I'll be forever indebted to those who, on the darkest of nights, brought me stars. You've saved my heart, soul and, in some cases, life — more times than you could know.

This book exists because of you.

Author's Note

Though my journey has not been easy, looking back, there seems to be an order to my life — Soul always guiding, tending, and quietly shaping the path toward her own unfolding.

The poetry and words in this book are small treasures redeemed from the hardest of those years. Sacred, initiatory, sometimes excruciatingly difficult years. Within them, however, I discovered a Self capable of holding sorrow, complexity, flaws and full humanity, as well as authentic beauty, compassion and acceptance — toward unfiltered joy. A vessel hollowed out enough for the divine to return, where life might become more deeply and vividly alive.

In retrospect, I see my path has been more about unlearning than learning. Untangling old scripts and constructs. Questioning what had been inherited from belief, society, schooling, lineage, and a culture that teaches us to forget our souls. Throughout it all, something deeper was always stirring, calling me Home. Calling me to remember an eternal song I had known innately as a child, not in words, but in the way feet trust the earth between their toes, or a heart knows the sun will rise after night. All before the world got in the way, and which I had only to Remember.

This book is the harvest, gathered by these raw, life-chafed hands, now offered into yours. I am a wanderer and a traveller returned to her village, my silhouette unrecognisable from the woman I was before. A soul many thought lost or beyond hope re-emerged, the dawn burning at her back, eyes shining, face radiant with soul's song.

I never intended my first published work to be one of poetry, yet my life became poetry —my journey toward soul its own story. For, as is always the way, soul has her own plans.

It is my hope that these pages fall open to the words or meditations you need now. Ones that might steady, nourish, or speak to your own hidden places. And perhaps, gently and in your own time, help return you to what you never truly lost: your own wholeness, and your soul's own magnificent, healing song. Just as they helped me.

With love and soul,
Rachel Alana (R.A. Falconer).

Contents

Soul Things	1
Courage	5
Permission	7
Free	11
Be	13
One Day	17
Wonder	19
Dark Birds	21
If We Saw Hearts	25
Beauty	29
Portraits	31
Too Often	37
Uprising	39
Dear Wisdom	43

Meeting	49
On Quiet Fields	51
Dearest Soul	53
Their Radiance	57
Here	61
It All	65
Light	67
Angels	71
Constellations	75
Cathedrals	77
Her Love	81
And Thus We Are	83
Forgive Yourself	85
How	89
Pole Star	91
Soul's Wild Hearth	95
Sing	97
Hold On	99
Such Whole Worlds	101
You're Not Alone	103

Bravely	105
Be Still	109
Stand	111
An Honour	115
Live Big!	117
Somehow	121
Walls	123
Be Authentic	125
Together	129
Return	133
Only	137
Concepts	141
Stars	143
The Story of Being	145
Leaves	151
Let the Aging Come	155
About The Author	167
Fullpage image	169
Fullpage image	171

Soul Things

A warm fire, crackling.
Falling rain. Broken bread.
An embrace.

A real smile.

A call with a friend and truly listening,
holding the space.
Not judging,
but waiting. Sharing tears.
Letting one another grow.

A sacred moment
of forgiveness.
A cat purring, curled upon a knee.

A burst of sunlight.
Body stretched out,
warmth on winter-pale skin.

First dawn
and the last bloom of dusk – to night.
Balmy nights and cold ones,
the kind that remind you you're alive.

Hearing the car and running footsteps.
Seeing those we've missed
for far too long —
or remembering them.

Laughter.
The thaw of grief.
Knowing that we loved,
or that someone, in all the crowd
saw us.

Weeping to the deep.
A sob, a gasp.
A bench wiped clean.
The scent of lemon. Of lavender.

Of tomorrow.

The roar of pain in birth
or in suffering.
Of someone holding your ugly,
your raw,
your lowest moment —
as though their own.

A sky full of stars.

Slow things.
Whole things.
Real things.

There,
where the TV is silent.
The house full of quiet,
or noise.
In presence, and in each other,
our holy Selves.

Before the buzz of doing
and having
convinced us

R.A. FALCONER

    there was some greater magic

      than simply being alive.

Courage

The greatest courage
is not to fight

but to *feel*.

Permission

You have permission to inhabit your own life.
To say no,
To say yes.
To inhabit your own Knowing.
Your own body.
And all you allow,
Or do not allow,
Within it.

To love who you love.
To feel.
To inhabit anger,
Contentment,
Joy,
And heavy sorrow.

To be full of strength,
And to know weakness.

Permission to stand for something,
Or to walk away.
To find rest. To tell your story.
To give or take what is yours,
And to never explain why you leave —
Or why you stay.

You have permission, grand permission
To have a voice — and to use it,
And to let others have theirs, too.
To add your voice to the Grand Mosaic,
Your brilliant tile to humanity,
And not be silenced.

You have permission to tell the truth,
And to let others tell theirs — or to be in quiet.
To choose to engage in the old wars ...
To win the game. To lose it.
Or to stand firm.
— Or to find something higher.

To know when not to listen,

Or when to be cracked open.
To let the silver spores of being infuse your life,
Or to watch your tender soul unfurl,
And come to flower.

You have permission to be Wild — so wild,
To live in, under, *to live through.*
To experience belief — and what it is to follow.
To lead,
Or to gather all you own, your whole being, if need be,
And take up your sacred path.

You have permission to live in your full truth today,
Even if that truth is gone tomorrow.
To be reborn.
Stunned like a babe, gasping from the womb —
Only to find rest in the warmth,
And soft breast
Of new Knowing.

You have permission to follow the call of your soul.
Even if it doesn't make sense.
Even if it is inconvenient.
Even if it only forms more questions.
Even if it only brings you freedom,

Or a heavy burden.

For you are not a herd beast.

You are a Being of Light,

Individuating your way out of the sleeping tribe.

You are an archangel, exalted to human,
Spreading the great arms of your wings
Into Life.

You are a Boat Builder,
A Clock Maker,
A Worker at the Compass,
Full of beauty, complexity,
And magnificent contradiction.

You, my dear,
Are a *Singer of the Soul*.

Never

Ever

Ask for permission.

Free

The tree does not say to the rock,
"You are unworthy."

The moon to the ocean,
"You are wrong.
You should not be."

The wind does not judge the fire.
The dry grass does not gossip
about the flea.

Yet we silly humans
have forgotten —
the sacred relief it is
just to be.

The world is whole
already.

Not much

is about you or me.

Be

Be kind to yourself.

Your heart,
and your dear body,
are always listening.

Give yourself a little space,
a little more slack.
No one can live in the tiny room
you've allowed for yourself.

Be gentle in your words.
Be generous and understanding.
For you are fashioned of the
dark, rich humus of this earth,

not only the lofty dust
of stars.

Catch those barbs and poisoned arrows
that you might think, or feel —
before they strike
that precious heart.

And send
those unloving thoughts
and doubts,
and the faulty worries
of this world —
away.

You're learning here.
You're growing.
And you're allowed to make
mistakes.

We all are.

And we will.

Your uniqueness,

and compassionate humanness
are needed in this injured world.

And we will only find true compassion
when we start ...

with our own
dear

selves.

One Day

One day you will rest into love.
One day, when it knocks, you will accept it
bravely, and without fear.
Open the door,
nod in recognition,
and let it in.

One day, you will fall
peacefully, my darling,
into trust.

One day,
when the curtains flutter out,
you'll draw them open,
consciously and completely.

Not because you are foolish,
but because you have been made wise.

Burned through to your true nature,
your unbreakable Self,
in life's dark fires.

One day, when you are ready,
you will hear the song of your soul.
And on that day,
when you reach the world's great towers,
they will mean nothing —
wholly and irretrievably.
And instead,
find yourself descending
into who you are.

One day, dear one, you will re-gather,
return. Re-member —
all of those lost treasures,
lost in love,
lost from trust ...
And rebirth them back to being

where they belong.

Wonder

Do you ever wonder
(I'm sure you do),
whatever happened to those dear souls
that we once knew?

Where are they now?
What stars aligned (or changed),
What paths or journeys did they lead?
What stayed the same?

Do you ever wonder
(I'm sure you do),
what became of those who left us,
or whom we just outgrew?

Who, for a while, became a world,
and left a vital spark.
Who played a lead
on life's brief stage,
a unique part.

Now, looking back,
we trace fate's wise and twining line.
And for good
or bad,
we honour them,
Their mark in Time.

Ah, the bittersweet experiences
and flow of life.

Where are you now,
once-friends,
once-lovers, colleagues,
forgotten foes?

We wish you well

... and only wonder.

Dark Birds

Dark birds of loss.
What sacred memories you unsettle
with your wings.
What hopes and loves
and entire worlds
scatter
to the wind.
The past never to return
beneath the same blue air.

These birds move on, and so must we.
Their lessons contained
in their slow, and eternal,
migrations.

For all souls must one day be set free.
Allowed to find the beauty
of another season's
clouds.
Their parting feathers catch stray beams of light,
gifting sudden smile,
leaving single tear.

Their secret language, gold warbles at half-light.
Hinting at wisdom — built of love,
mistakes. 'If onlys'
(far too many 'if onlys')
Memories tumbled feathers
amongst the grass.

But even as they move on,
do not despair.
For new birds always come to settle
on life's branches.

Greeting us with somehow familiar eye,
Different birds.
Some changed.
The scent of whole other lands
upon their wings.

Ready to build new nests.
Ready to endow new songs.

So as regrets and loss touch us
with their parting chorus —
be comforted.

For we too, will one day fly as birds.
Alighting
into new seasons.
New loves.
Transformed lives.

With rolling zephyrs, an endless swell
beneath our wings,

ever ready to turn course —

toward Life's soft, and glancing light
of dawn.

If We Saw Hearts

Imagine if we celebrated people
not for how beautiful they looked,
but for how beautifully they lived.

Not for being the richest,
but for how they made life easier,
kinder,
for the people around them.

Not for looking younger than their age,
but in growing the wiser for it.

Not for achieving the most,
but for walking through it all,
the real stuff,

and staying open.

Imagine if we got curious
about the fine print of someone's life —
Their dreams.
How they move through the world,
how they do a thing they love.
What calls their soul ...

What if school taught us
not just how to break things down —
numbers, facts, theories, history —
but how to build connection?

How to be a good friend,
partner,
parent,
human.
How to stay connected
to our dreams.
To ourselves.

Imagine if we really saw
the tender hearts
we share this life with:

the partner offering
the best years of their life.
The child
with the wide, searching eyes.
The friend, or grandparent,
we keep meaning to call.

What if we saw them
with the same care and reverence
we give to a job, a house,
a deadline,
a reputation?

What if we treated hearts
like heirloom china,
or a rare piece of art ...
not something to fix after it breaks,
but something to protect
and handle gently
from the start?

Wouldn't it be a different kind of world
if we didn't turn away
from the sadness in a child's eyes,
the silence of a friend,

the ache in our own chest?

If we understood,
really understood,
that hearts are sacred.

And something much
much, much harder to replace

than anything else
in this world.

Beauty

Beauty is a shadow in this world.
Her touch
lifting life
through city concrete.
Her voice
cooing poems
through traffic's hum.

Be still
(and you will find Her).

... She's trailing Magic
behind the sun.

Portraits

People will judge you.
Not much can be done
about that.

Some will misunderstand.
Some will misrepresent you,
(it's sad,
but true).

There will be those who try
to hold you too still.

Make you fit,
press you down,
lock you into

some old story,
told too often
behind closed doors.
Left on repeat
in long abandoned
rooms.

Portraits,
frozen in time,
pinned crooked on peeling walls,
gathering dust in back corners.
In places you so long ago
outgrew.

And yet,
even as your ghost haunts
those liminal
and mirrored hallways,
dancing out a thousand lives
you never lived.
A thousand crimes
they can't forgive ...

you must carry on.

Even as your name
is passed from mouth to mouth,
tasted and slowly turned over
like some foreign wine.
As though they know you ...
As though they've seen
the vast,
submerged ice
beneath the ocean's skin ...

keep going.

A life of trying on roles:
villain, saint,
victim, fool (so many times fool),
king, queen,
sinner,
damsel-in-distress—

as though their words might
make you small enough
to understand —
*Like boxing in
the deep blue sea.*

But these projections
are no more You
than a memory
in a half-remembered dream.
They may have offered you a cloak at times
(or many) —

But dear one, in life's strange,
and static galleries,
where people try to capture
these precious
human lives,
there exists some desperate hope to own
what cannot be owned.
To know
what cannot be known.
And to judge another

lest they face themselves.

But tips of icebergs have a habit of sinking
even the grandest ships.

So, whatever happens,

don't be contained,
dear friend.
Don't reduce yourself
to fit
their narrow frames.

Wear the cloak
(if it suits you).
And when it doesn't,
like a dog soaked through
from heavy rain,

shake it free.

You were never meant
to be a portrait on a shelf.
A relic kept behind glass.
A single story frozen
in time.

No.
You are *Vast*.
You are *Unfolding* ...

and you are a Mystery

Still-Becoming.

You, dear one,

are *You.*

Too Often

Too often the Great Ones
come dressed as beggars

While devils
come cloaked as kings.

Uprising

When the world forgets its sacredness.
When everything is reduced
to resource,
to profit,
to possession —

There are those
who embroider time
with weaving fingers,
And who invite you
into life's sacred
moments.

Who dream of peace, with dove.
And flow with life's currents, like turtle.

Planting sorrows in deep soil
to wait for spring.

Who stand beneath the stars
with the still, black sea
at night.

Those who have known hardship.
Who have stood in the furnaces of life,
and let them temper,
not destroy, them.

Those who have been scraped to the marrow
by trials,
by unfairness, by suffering,
and still —
who still, *still* —
choose love.

These are the ones who remind us.
And though they are not many,
they are enough.

They play with bare feet
on the royal robes

of the Earth.
Press their palms to Her heart,
drink in Her sunsets,
revere Her essence,

and Listen.

They know how to call back the Soul.
They know Her drumbeat,
the dust-path,
the guttural prayer.
The Aliveness
of it all.

"Remember where you are," they whisper.
"Remember what this world is.
You are here only a short time,
but one so important.
The thread to Memory is never lost—
only frayed.

'Walk until your feet recall the earth.
Breathe, until your breath
tastes Her fragrant, nourishing air
again ...

And look,
look —
until you see the soul once more before you,
in all its glorious beauty."

These are the Ones of Life.
Of every bloodline, songline,
nation,
name.

Some call them "rebels,"
but they are far greater.

They are Life
and its Remembering—

Soul's quiet and magnificent
Uprising.

Dear Wisdom

Dear Wisdom,
I have come to understand
something
of your Song.

You are not either/or,
nor for/or against.

You are not, "Your enemy is my friend,"
nor, "Your falsehood
makes the opposite
true."

This can be hard to understand
in this split, bipolar

and divisive world.

But your language breaks through
sparks of shattering light.
A mosaic built of times and seasons,
of both left and right,
man and woman,
deep dark and searing light.
And every inspiring colour
of imagination
in between.

Your hand moves low to gently push
each chess piece and play each note.
That, Wisdom, is your rich paradox
and sacred music.

Your ever-sorting of the wheat from the chaff
is your ear to Life,
and the true Seeing of it.

Responding not from unthinking beliefs,
or collective madness,
but rather, with
Exactly-What-Is-Needed

Right Now.

You are Insight's sudden gasp,
and understanding distilled
to its pure essence.

The nourishing balm
that soothes the troubled brow.
The Truth that finds footing
through a world of turbulent seas.
The Gold to mend a numbed
or broken heart.

Dear Wisdom,
You are the moonlight-reveal,
through parting cloud
illuminating the path.

And the arms that soothe, with softened gaze
to reassure: "I've been there too."

You know the way — sometimes the only salve
through Dark Nights
without end.

You are born of the fainter paths,
the harder roads, the deeper valleys.
Those that are never the most direct way —
but find the depths.

Wisdom,
You are the reward of a full life.
A ripened field heavy with promise
into Abundant Light.
The sacred endowment
of the human experience.

Falls and mistakes,
living,
are your only (and greatest),
price.

Stitched with silver into histories
to be inherited by generations,
each then, to inevitably
add their own
unique thread.

You come through tears and hell-journeys.
Through broken lives and dreams and losses.

Rarely heavens.

But, if held truly,
you pay the worker
with the greatest bread.

Dear Wisdom,
perhaps we only hear your whisper
at 3 a.m.,
but it speaks directly:

"I am why you are here. And the only thing,
(Everything),
you may take with you."

Guiding the bewildered,
the humbled, and Life's
Lost
Travellers

Home.

Meeting

God found another in a face,
for just a moment.

Divinity in a laugh,
a universe in shared pain.

Union
in the catch of eyes,

gently meeting.

On Quiet Fields

Nature has no position.
The cool, grey wind,
The blue and scented trees —
None call you by name.
Nor does Nature know
of your wrongdoings.

The crumbling dirt
knows nothing of your successes.
The opening blooms
nothing of your failures,
your pain,
even your grief.

Neither does the storm that breaks black thunder

know of your titles,
your ideas, your categories,
your possessions,
or your long and well-worn righteousness —

Who the world says *You are.*

In the arms of the green wave and endless grasslands.
In the breath of eucalyptus and chilled pine —
And in the weave of winding vine
and clear, rushing river —
our mistakes fall loose, like dust.
Our beliefs and dreams are washed free,
like dirt from skin.

Our Hearts, our Souls
and True Voice
Remembered.

A Crow's long cawing upon the wind.

Dearest Soul

When my mind is quiet,
and I forget the blast of definitions of this world
(and the low smoke clears) ...

I'll free fall
down ...

Down ...

Past the dragons and the darkness,
the briars and thorned hedges,
(called The Old Stories).

Past the fluttering veils,
and the towering walls

(of Learned Defences).
— Into the depths
where I hear Your voice,
calling.
(Find Me).

Down ...

Until there,
at the bottom of
despair's dark
well,
I catch Your stillness in the mirror.

I find You standing
at those moon-milk windows
(called my eyes).

You take my hand,
our touch like the promise
of first daffodils
through snow.

And like secret friends
we explore our sacred being.

It's hidden rooms and deep,
ancestral oceans ...
where dreams thought lost
appear again
like ghosts.

Old pains in nooks and memories tangled.
Cobwebs.
(And buried treasure).

And there,
in the mid-night swells of Your embrace,
I finally see

Me.

Not harsh words, not wounds,
nor criticism,
or sadness —
But our own Divinity, Soul.

And in the Seeing, our great wings expand,
our proud chest lifts
(in Joy. In Love),

And tears, wild with seasons,
brake across our eyes …
To nourish branches, to weave out worlds,
this heart unfurling.
I love You, Woman in the mirror.

My precious Soul, where have you been?
And these lips whisper back:

Birthing Life.

Come with Me.

Their Radiance

Sometimes,
we meet those who radiate love
like sunlight.
Offering warmth,
and asking
nothing.

They live with purpose
as gardeners might.
Hands deep in the earth,
tending life with wise,
and gentle
attention.

Around them,

things grow.
People grow.
Souls unfold.

We forget
how rare it is
to be near such light.
But there are few things
as blessed.

Keepers
of Life's great, Heirloom seeds
endowed with names
like:

Steadfastness.
Compassion.
Truth-telling.
Sacred listening.
Courage.
Devotion.

Guided, tended,
watered,
pruned with love

toward soul's sweet
and greatest
expression.

Here,
with such Centred and radiant beings
we are found again in blossom.
Full

of the vivid, miraculous
hues *of love,*
of hope,

of our Truest Selves.

I have called myself blessed
to fall within the orbit
of such people.

Nourished.
Steadied.
Believed in —

and sustained toward Soul's wholeness ...

by loving Radiance.

Here

You are the soft touch
of your own centre.
The sweet kiss
of your own lips.

The hearted night,
the moonlit vestibule.
The mellow
and foreign
darkness.

Do you know me?
Will you?

This desert,

swift with burning sands,
shifts and glides
to encircle life's deep
centre.

My own soul, still raw,
heart beating,
nestles safe
against my chest.
Oh, this magnificent, yet fragile bird.

Though new, this bird is wild.
She opens one gold eye,
which pierces – discerning, soft,
fierce, like Falcon.

Her view is aligned and self-determined,
and she is ready.

Ready
to show me the lay of the land.
Ready
to heed my call.

I will not hand you recklessly to civilisation,

Soul,
nor to anyone else,
in some fleeting hope
of validation.

There is no need. For you are here.
Returned to me.
Alive.

We are wholeness.

We are here.

It All

I never quite fit in,
and at first,
that brought me grief.

Until I found Soul's
Unique Self...

— And then

*it all became
a gift.*

Light

Do not lose your light.

Even when things feel uncertain,
and the dawn forgets to come,
do not lose your fire.
Hold close
your inner sun.

Do not lose your fire,
and do not lose your light,
for it's in the inner tending,
the eternal soul
burns bright.

Do not lose your light.

Nor hand its sacred tending
to the changing figures
of the night.

Do not lose your light.

And, as things grow darker
(or longer, or the days colder),
know it's in the sharing
that more brilliant lamps
ignite.

Do not lose your light.

For even in great storm or drought,
or darkness,
the lamp of the soul
is bright.

Hold close to your light.
For no outer force can steal it.
The light of soul — it always embers

through the Darkest
of all Nights.

Do not lose the light.

(You cannot lose the Light).

Angels

Perhaps you are an angel here,
and lost your wings along the way.

You know who you are.

You know because you sense the old ache
just there, below the neck.

The phantom imprint
of the sweeping wingspan.
The ghost of a great, lost expanse ...

in the tiny office cubicle.
In the difficult marriage.
In the lost moments, the impossible situations,

the heavy and irreconcilable
places.

You know they were once there,
because sometimes
you still feel them.

An urge to fly away.
To find a more rarefied air —
But also,
perhaps more strongly,

you feel them unfolding in great arcs
as though from nowhere,
as you meet the woman they judge —
poor, or drunk,
or lost,
and offer out a compassionate hand.

Not because you feel sorry for her,
but because
you recognise the sheared edges of life
from which her own sodden
and broken wings
could not save her —

and you call her Sister.

Perhaps, as you lie in the dark,
you feel the writhe of your own lost wings,
seeking freedom.
Wondering how to go on.
How to live in a foreign land.
How to fly,
in a world too heavy for wings —
In a world that needs
light.

And perhaps,
like the hint of lost wings,
you also remember your Song here.
Why it is so.
And that you are not lost,
but an angel

fallen.

Here to know the ground, the beautiful mud
and humbling dirt.
The messy reality of things.

Where,
in love and life, we might finally restore
our own lost wings.
And become our own,
and one another's,
angels.

All these Earth angels, you and I,

of lost wing and feather.

Constellations

Why would you define
the entire universe
that is You

by
one
small

star?

Cathedrals

Take my hand,
we have found ourselves
in the Cathedral.
A jewel of shining sapphire
in an otherwise inhospitable universe.

Be still,
we have remembered
we are here.

A rare place,
where days, like coins, spread gold
and amber,
and city lights gleam
as continents turn their burning altars

through the night.

Here, storms gloam and shadow,
and grasses bow in fields
upon their knees.

Do you hear Her hymns?
The ice singing over frozen lake.
The hush and roar
of flowing ocean.

Do you hear Her whales?
See the swirling birds ascend in prayer
through white visions
of ghostly mist?

We had almost forgotten.

Replaced the Real with cheap fad
and empty trinket.
With prestige and hollow idol,
with endless doing
to fill the void –
as we clear-cut voids
into hallowed ground.

But hush ...
listen.
Beneath the dome
and brilliant tapestry of sky,
the scales are falling.

Beneath the pinnacle of mountain,
and steepled spires of ancient forest ...

Through the sermon
of changing seasons,
and under baptismal rain.

In Her untamed storms
and within Her rough, dark clay

we find redemption.

For Nature has no position.

She was here before us,
and will be here
long after.

And from distanced supplications,

we have finally woken
to find our souls undone
to Life.
Her closed vaults open.

And in Her Cathedrals,
we see — no,
we *Remember.*

Our dear Earth,
and the sweetest Heaven,

were always one.

Her Love

Her love was like clean water,
and abundance.

Like crisp air,
and the dark, sprawling arms
of forest.

Like birdsong at dawn,
and the sweet, fertile creations
of bees.

Always there,
and barely noticed.

Until,

one day,

it all was gone.

And Thus We Are

We think —
therefore,
we exist.

We love,
listen,
dream, laugh
connect, *sense, experience,*
yearn, cry,
breathe,
give —

feel ...

And thus,
we are

Alive.

Forgive Yourself

Forgive yourself
for what you had to do to survive.
Forgive yourself for who you were
before you knew better.

Forgive yourself
for being fallible, broken,
for being less than perfect.

Touch the earth
in your small humanness.
Feel the dirt beneath your feet,
between your fingers,
and how your tears water
the parched, cracked soil.

Forgive yourself
for not being more,
for not knowing more,
for learning through experience,
or the hard way.

For what you did to survive life's winters,
across life's thin ice.
For your mistakes.

You survived.
You are here.

And in the forgiveness,
let your hands reach down
to soothe your own broken heart,
and from there,
the broken hearts of others.

For we grow humble in our falls,
compassionate through our imperfection,
not our perfection.

Forgive yourself.
Let the weight of these lessons

hold you firmly
in their dark wisdom
to the earth —

And from there,
like a sky of shining lanterns,

set your soul free.

How

So easily we see
the holes
in how we were loved —

and not, dear one,
in how we loved.

Pole Star

Sometimes there is a sudden drop of wind.
The sails flap a little,
collapse,
and the dark seas
grow still.

For mile upon grey mile, the blue sky is filled
with an endless Silence.

Even terrible storms,
the kind the hardened sailors of life
meet with dread,
stir the dark waves.

Even rip-tides, reefs, great perilous swells

and churning currents,
(as treacherous and challenging as they might be),
propel a woman's boat swiftly
across the water.

But Silence?

Silence offers nothing,
and yet, in its sheer yawning power,
everything.

'Who are you?' It whispers from the black depths,
from that great endless womb,
of waiting ocean.

The Silence lengthens. Gapes to hours ...

Days,
Weeks.

'What Trade Winds swell your sails?'

And in the stillness,
where blank sky meets the lightless waters,
where up meets down and left, right,

and swirling brine
finds translucent light.

All touch gently at the edges,
merging into One —

a pole star beaming bright through parting clouds,

'The Soul demands its journey,'
comes the fearsome whisper.

And fast as that great God descended,
Life's winds roar back full force
in their return,
new waves surging beneath the hull.

And all you can hope,
as you grapple for the spinning helm,
is to meet life
with more authentic answers,

born of sacred depths
on long and beautiful seas

of Waiting, Rest,

and Reflection.

— And steer the new course
set by Soul.

Soul's Wild Hearth

Tell me not:

What you do,
nor, *Where you live,*
nor, *Who you are*
in these dull,
cement constructions
of this world.

But rather,

Tell me,
What it is you love.
What brings your heart back
to searing joy.

What sorrows and hard lessons
you wouldn't change —
even if you had
the chance to,

and all you have learned
in this one,
rare life.

Tell me, dear friend,

Where the wisdom
of your wild, soul's hearth

has brought you.

Sing

Speak
until you are ready to find the Silence.
Find Silence
until you are ready to Speak.

Be Silent
until the words have seeded
and nestled deep in the dark.

Been nourished and enriched
by the Power of Life,
by Sorrow's Tears,
and by the Lessons you have won
through sheer grit
and the will to survive.

Through endurance,
and determination.

And there,
there,
having reached the culmination
of this life-dark place, and brave,
such brave
gestation —

Be Ready, dear one.

For every caged bird, caught by Life's
sometimes near-impossible trials,
its high walls,
and seemingly insurmountable
restrictions,
must learn

Finally

to spread the mighty Wisdom of Her Wings

and *Sing*.

Hold On

Sometimes, it can be no more than this:

Hold on, hold on

Hold on.

Such Whole Worlds

It is hard to believe
that some people
who were in life, or in love
everything to us
are gone.

A dream of turning veils
folded now into the rich soil of the past.
Lost to life's chapters
only to be found changed
at each rereading.
Essence fading
with each turning page.

As rocks wear to sand,

As trees, alive and powerful, fall to wood,
consumed to ash.
As long storms clear,

It is hard to imagine
that such whole worlds
once our everything,

Disappear.

You're Not Alone

Even during your lowest moments,
when you feel nothing but clay against the dark earth,

you are never alone.

You have thousands of powerful ancestors behind you.
Those who have lived
through life's wilds
and wastelands,
griefs and hardships.
And do so
with you now.

They carry you
in the gnarled and knotted embrace

of the Tree of Life.
Each bestowing a dark seed of promise
in the ripe,
waiting ground
of your sleeping cells.

Feel their proud voices, their dreams for you,
and their advice
like moonlight.

Feel the loving hands that lift you
from the edges of despair
or bewilderment,
into clarity.

Hear their wisdom —
That it is the journey that matters,
and the success
lies in simply taking it ...

As they return you gently to your feet,

and into the life you came here to live.

Bravely

You must go bravely
into your own life
and find the truth of it.

Go bravely into this world,
for it awaits
your unique place.

Go bravely
toward your pain,
and felt resistance.

Bravely into the depths,
into all you lost,
gave up, or buried,

to survive life's race.

Go bravely
toward the song of your soul.
Do not let it grow quieter
with each passing year.

And though you'll hear a lot of voices,
still,
go bravely.

Do not forget the reason
you are here.

Land bravely
in the place your heart
calls sacred soil.

And there
lay glistering sparks
that bear your Name.

It doesn't matter
if they become
gentle star,

or blazing supernova ...

Tend each with presence,
into your sacred claim.

Go bravely
beyond your past,
and the stories
that bind you.

Bravely
beyond the false calls
of silver, gold,
and shadowed truth.

Go bravely, my friend,
toward soul,
so bravely.

No path will ever ask,
(nor reward so Grandly),

the all of You.

BE STILL

Your soul

has become a roar.

Stand

The way through to self-acceptance
is not in more exercise,
more diets,
more products,
nips, tucks,
or "reversals of time".
Or in the riches
to afford such.

Rather,

It's in sitting
with that lost, abandoned,
taunted
and despised
dragon of shame.

At our own inheritance,
and humbling,
human imperfection.

At all we find wrong
about ourselves,
or want to change.

At the wild and rugged landscapes
we'll then uncover,
of our own being.

At our uniqueness.
At the certain strides
toward ageing, wisdom,
and the comfort in the
slow unfolding
toward Self.

At this rare,
strange and wonderful
Human condition,

and learning not just to *love,*

but
to stand

in

awe.

An Honour

Wisdom
will have Her way.

She will not let you return
from this war

without wearing
her battle-scars
with honour.

Live Big!

Oh! She is too big,
too thin,
too old,
too young.
Her nose too small,
too large, too short, too straight,
and, oh dear,
(I don't mean to be rude),
but not quite in the middle.

Her eyes too close, wait, too wide set.
Neck too long? No, not long enough.
Jaw too strong, too narrow.
Too timid.
Too loud.

With voice too high
or not high enough at all.

And did I mention her waist?
Her legs? Her bust, her bottom,
her big ideas?
Her daring
to show herself outside at all?

Oh, please, just stop all that.
For life's too short (and far too grand),
to dissect, destroy,
with self-limiting demands.

Live big instead!
Live bright,
with joy and free.
This unique vessel
is soul's precious home a time,
— in you, in me.

For many a magnificent forest
was brought to ash,
and crashed down to lumber.
Great wonders reduced to chip and block

by those who slumber.

So, through embodied
heart and soul,
may we all bloom and thrive,
fruit and flower.

By living from life's deeper Self,
may we find instead

True Beauty's
Unmatched Power.

Live Big!

Somehow

Somehow,

through the noise of expectations,

past all we do

to earn,

to prove,

to be worthy,

loved

we'll finally find

again

the voice
of our own heartbeat.

Walls

Walls keep us safe
they keep the world out.

A whole, wide world out.

Be Authentic

Be Authentic
About needing help.
About being human.
About sometimes getting angry.
About sometimes needing to cry.

Be Authentic.
That we haven't always got it all together.
That we don't always know the answers.
That we've failed spectacularly in some things,
and risen mightily to the occasion
in others ...

And that's okay.

Be Authentic.
For Here We Are,
having this strange, this sad, sacred
and beautiful Human Experience.
Though sometimes we're told we need to be Gods,
Goddesses,

but we're not.

Instead, we age. Get ill. Get round, thin. Poor,
Proud, frail. Imperfect.
Sometimes we Fail.
And that's how it's meant to be.

So, dear one,
breathe.

Be Authentic.
It's not about letting ourselves go,
but rather, letting ourSelves 'Be'.
Finding Rest in the arms of Self,
restoring ourselves back
to the simple Beauty of this Life.

Be Authentic.

For sometimes we get lost
in the too much refining,
the too much trying, the too much saccharine
perfection.
But our tastebuds for Life can come back —
they truly can.

And not just taste Life again,
but find Joy.

Be Authentic.
Real.
For it's all a process of Sacred Growing.
That we might take this beautiful
and rare Life —
this Journey —
together.

Until we finally come to meet each other again,
ourselves,
the world even,
at the greatest, and yet most simple place
of all ...

That is:

R.A. FALCONER

The *Where We Are At*

Right Now.

Together

Tell me
everything they mistake as you.
Everything that offered the template,
the outline, until you knew its borders,
its hard edges,
its not-you-ness.

Tell me all the thousand things,
the verbs that became nouns.

I want to know where you were born,
what school you went to,
what qualifications
come after your name.

I want to know what they call you —
if it matters,
if it's important, or not important.
Who you vote for,
your colour, your sexuality, your job.
What illness they named you,
what religion you are,
the page number you match
in the *DSM-5*.

I want to see how you say it.
How your eyes light up,
or if you look away.
If you think it's you, or not —
like being the new dress,
or naming yourself
after the car.

I want to know what bridges to cross.
What walls I need to climb.
How thick the hedges are
they've clipped so neat
around you, me —
to be able to reach
Who We Really Are …

behind the defences,
behind the identifications.

So then, Together,
under such incredible constellations,
we can meet

as two bare and simple Souls,

and be Real.

Return

You can feel the press of the coming tsunami
behind the gaze
of some souls.

The building pressure
of eons.
The great dams
held back.

The drawn tide of silenced voices,
waiting
behind glistening eye.
Behind the slight flinch,
of stilled lips.

Lives chewed up by The Machine
lay bare upon the sand.

Too many beautiful dreams lost.
Too many hearts broken.
Too many stories
disallowed.

Great Leaders and the truly Strong
elevate.
They do not crush.

Those who take power
to aggrandise only themselves
will eventually lose it.

The sea has pulled back to become a towering wave.
A wild, soulful and magnificent border,
growing
at the horizon.

Justice waits upon the tongue.
Built on the salt of Losses,
Lessons, Sacrifices ...

A mighty wall unswayed,
as the Voice of Life
rises fearless,
toward Heaven.

The sand

glares

white.

We hear Her rumble.

Only

Only a fool
would tell a mighty tree
it was too old.

Only a fool
would tell the great dunes they had too many lines,
the natural brush
too many wind-rippled grooves.

Only a fool
would tell the ocean, the silverback,
the majestic albatross
they had gone too grey.
Or reduce flourishing gold field
to the appearance

of a layer of topsoil.

Only a fool
would chase a single season of life.
Seeing no more than the new buds of spring,
or the abundance of life's summers —
ignoring the vast colour,
stillness, movement,
and breath-taking grandeur
in them all.

Only a fool
would not live
from the time-lived Wisdom
of the Heart.

For it is this earned
and sacred Lens
that can perceive such Wonder
and such Beauty.

And, sadly,
this exact lack
that makes all too many in this world

a fool.

Concepts

Beware of those
with no inner-life,
for you too
will be
reduced
to an object,

a surface of things,
a concept,
a category
and consumable ...

*in the World
of Things.*

Stars

*The whole universe
conspires in your favour
when you decide
to live your sacred path.*

*Watch the dark clouds part —
the fog dry to naught,*

*and the Soul's
passage forward*
appear.

*The way
twinkling to sacred shape,*

R.A. FALCONER

... under burning stars.

The Story of Being

Life offers us changes.

It might feel like an end to the world,
but there is no end,
not really —
Only new places, new vistas to see
and to experience.

Sometimes it is hard
and we wonder how we got here.
Which doors we took,
which ones we were meant,
or never meant
to open.

But it isn't in the doubting,
or in the questioning —
But rather,
it's in the full inhabiting
of one's life.

The standing in where we are —
With the wind in our face,
the sun bright against our skin,
and the darkness always at the horizon,
waiting.

Here, we can take up the pen
and begin to write our own story.

Perhaps it will be a comedy.
Maybe a tragedy.
As we step wholly into the pages of our life,
what will it be?

Perhaps we were idiots,
or were betrayed.
Maybe we became full of pride
or victimhood.
Maybe we became lost, or grew full

of our own importance.

Perhaps we were masters for a time —
fell in love, joy, bliss,
grief,
or into madness.
Maybe we made errors of judgment
whose hard lessons we now must learn,
or must pay for.

Or maybe, maybe,
there is a harvest.
Shining rich and golden
as we step up to the precipice,
ready to gather its fragrant wheat
into our arms,
after so many long years
of waiting.

This is Life.
And Life awaits our presence — not our safety,
not our hesitation.

Between life's hard covers,
from Her transformations,

Her beginnings, to Her end,

Smile.
Embrace.
Give.

Do not live in fear,
even as they tell us
that is all there is.

Laugh.
Even in the darkness.
Even in the question.
Even in Her tears.

Live.
For we are here a short time,
and maybe it is a tragedy.
Maybe it is an opera
(or just a grand comedy).
Or perhaps,
perhaps the story stands as a spectacular fall from grace,

But do not let it be nothing.

All these things mark our place in Time,
and are initiations into Wisdom.

Live it (don't be afraid), and live it grandly,
even the mistakes,
even the cold and the lost alleyways.
Even if it means knowing that one slip
and our soul may go home.
(For one day, our soul must go Home.)

The Great Book of our Life
must be our life.
The Great Story of Being, our own.

Read it. Breathe it.
Write it.

Turn off the fear on the television,
and turn in love
to those around you.

For this here is our Story,
every page, every spark,
every word.
Breath.

For to our Souls,
every moment is *Fire*.

LEAVES

Did you ever really own
the dirt beneath your feet?
The home you lost.
The ones who left you?

Did you ever really own
the child who grew up
and went away?

The job that moved you on?
The things you broke,
The worlds burned down?

Things borrowed,
stolen,

or never returned?

— The lover
who with such tender kiss
betrayed you?

Did you ever really own
the land you called your home?
The dust
where a million other feet
broke paths before?

'Come home.'
This whisper, so like the breeze,
runs low through leaves,
through deepening forest.

'To what is yours.
Come Home,
to your own Land,
and Soul's Own Country.'

You lift a hesitant hand to test the wind.
Your body stirs,
Soul's voice a soothing balm

across the skin.
Rich songs, familiar stirrings
beneath the ribcage.

'Lay claim to this wild universe,
and this small,
yet sacred vessel
that contains it.

For on this Stone,
Soul will not walk away,
nor leave you.
Nor be lost,
stolen,
taken away.

Not, once it has been found.'

And with aching heart,
you hoist that rusted anchor free ...
With strengthening arms,
you raise hope's billowing sails.

Brave and true,
for it's you.

Glorious You.

All else leaves upon the wind.

'Come now,' Soul whispers,
the sound a silver thread
across the dark.
'A land soul never left,

Come now,

*I will carry you
Home.*'

Let the Aging Come

As you bow proudly
to receive this seasoned Cloak of Life,
you are found to have earned
every line and stitch.
Your life-story expanding great albatross wings,
across closing dusk.

You tracked the footprints of this unique woman.
Became acquainted
with her ways.
Knew her in the way
you hoped a parent might,
or a lover,
or a dear friend.

Her whys and hows, her gifts,
and her many faults.
You watched her view of life wax
and wane,
only to realise, at last,
she was your greatest,
though most difficult
Love.

And now,
as you lower your head to accept
this burnished wreath
of autumn leaves,
you find they do not fade but glower
with intense
and growing ember.

An unforgettable flare
toward life's final scene,
as the sun dips from one horizon —
only to rise
defiant,
upon another.

These intricate

caverns of being
have been mapped out
to their edges.
The ice of endless, wintery nights
have been found transformed —
to sparkling jewels.

The fruits and foliage of life's harvests
are plucked down
to their bare branches.
Stored away.
Their essence tended
to be tasted, many times over
in soul's eternal storehouse.
This sacred chiaroscuro
of a Life.

So let the Aging come.
For it is a privilege denied many,
and a culmination
into deeper Beauty.

For you have journeyed
life's hard roads
and lived to tell the tale

of jagged pathways,
roadmaps recorded in calligraphy
upon the skin.

Streams of joy. Tracks of sorrow.
Excesses and suffering.
And quiet spring glades, noondays,
decades —
all held now
in the bottomless archives
of your eyes.

You have lived out whole worlds,
and built lives from scratch
with your own hands,
and the help of others.
Births. Deaths. Losses.
Revelations.
Love.
And the surviving of it all.
Shirtsleeves rolled to elbows.
Countless tears washed free
with summer rains.

So let the Aging come.

These greying tresses now flow free
as you turn back to witness
the powerful, silver currents
of a life.

And at the precipice
of new-flowered meadows
you watch the world turn right-side round.
And discover,
you were only a traveller
here for a while.
That the time comes always,
to return from this strange
and shallow dream,
to Home.

Let the Aging come.

For you have fought life's wars,
and the old scars still ache
on quiet nights.

You've lived for love
and without it,

and fought against it.

Danced the old tunes.
Took the easier roads,
and the steeper, the foolish,
the more stupid paths.
Experienced the bottomless, unyielding waters
of grief,
and yowled anger
at unhearing skies.

So,
let it come.

You have carried yourself with dignity.
And landed face-first, in the mud.
Worn the burden of blame,
of shame,
and been the larger, in forgiveness.

— Been the more rigid
in judgment.

And carried the unlived-lives of others,
only to bend the finger, finally,

toward your own.

May it come.

For through it all,
as these shadows stretch long
toward approaching dusk,
you find this frail and calloused body
grow tender,
and be made more humble.
More real,
and more Beautiful
by Life.

And now,
as the light shifts its eternal quality,
you feel the songs
of these approaching clouds.
And in their reflection
see that it all worked to conspire
toward a wilder flowering,
as you leave the layers
of false care and worry
behind.

And with each stripping away
comes an incredible freedom
and an Eternal Flame.
One that glows,
and can never wane or die,
within.

For we grow wild in our loss,
strong in the silence
of our winters.
Love will always break her rays,
through hallowed ground.

So now,
in this lowering light and chapter,
Let this soul find peace
in the gnarled,
the lined,
the mottled,
and the bristling,
the creaking,
And in the clarity
and slow vanishing
of this false
and impermanent dream.

And here
you find yourself
at The Great Beginning.

Ready.

For you are a worthy Vessel
of a small
and precious Story
in Time.

An Infinite Soul
in the evolving Beauty

and Poetry

between all Things.

Dedicated to my children.

The four chambers of my heart.

ABOUT THE AUTHOR

Rachel Alana (R.A. Falconer) is an Australian poet, writer, and curator of the popular Facebook and Instagram page *Midwives of the Soul*. Born in the New South Wales border town of Albury, she now lives in Adelaide, South Australia — its long white beaches, red dirt, and lush foothills an endless story to her soul and heart.

Her poetry has been shared widely across social media platforms with tens of thousands of shares; with translations by readers into languages including French, Spanish, German, Romanian and Polish.

She is the mother of four grown children whom she adores, and shares her home with two cats, several chickens, and two guinea pigs.

Three more poetry anthologies — *Soul Stories*, *Soul Balms* and *Ruminations* — are in the works.

SOUL SONGS

www.ingramcontent.com/pod-product-compliance
Lightning Source LLC
Chambersburg PA
CBHW060356080526
44583CB00012B/337